THE SIRHOWY VALLEY

AS IT WAS and AS IT IS

Volume 1

Ewart Smith

Old Bakehouse Publications

Abertillery

First published in November 2003

ISBN 1 874538 13 1

Published in the U.K. by
Old Bakehouse Publications
Church Street,
Abertillery, Gwent NP13 1EA
Telephone: 01495 212600 Fax: 01495 216222
Email: oldbakehouseprint@btopenworld.com

Made and printed in the UK
by J.R. Davies (Printers) Ltd.

British Library Cataloguing in Publication Data: a catalogue record for this book is available from the British Library.

Contents

Foreword

by

County Borough Councillor Angus Donaldson MBE

formerly County Councillor for Monmouthshire and Gwent,
and former Mayor of the Borough of Caerphilly

Ewart has done it again. This is his fifth book on local history and is a must for people who live in the valley however old they may be. Ewart and I met in Tredegar more than forty years ago when we were catering for the needs of two quite different groups of inhabitants! Several books have been published about Tredegar, Blackwood and the associated villages, but this is the first to take such a broad sweep of the whole length of the Sirhowy Valley both 'As it was' and 'As it is'. Ewart stood at sixty different sites in the valley during the summer of 2003. At those sites he photographed what can be seen today. These are then compared, on facing pages, with what stood on each site in the past - sometimes almost a hundred years ago. I found turning these pages very nostalgic and was made to appreciate how much things have changed. In many instances the two photographs are totally unrecognisable as being taken from the same spot. The deep-mine collieries at Ty Trist, Pochin, Bedwellty Pits, Markham, Oakdale, The Rock, Wyllie and Nine Mile Point, and the many other small collieries and levels have all disappeared. Nature, with a little help from man, has reclaimed these sites so that it is difficult to accept, in some cases, that a colliery ever stood there. The railways and their stations have also disappeared. Tredegar, where I spent a large fraction of my life looking after the Castle Hotel, stands like a sentinel at the head of the valley. The town is totally changed from the days when thousands of men worked in the iron works, brickworks and collieries.

Ewart must be thanked for bringing this collection of photographs together. It reminds us of what life used to be like and helps us to appreciate how much things have improved for the working people of this valley. Our valley is steeped in social and industrial history and it is only through the efforts of people such as Ewart that this history is kept alive in photographs. This enables us to compare life in the past with life today. I am very happy to be associated with such an interesting book and wish Ewart every success with this, his latest publication.

Introduction

Change is one of the certainties of life. We change our looks, sometimes for the better but sometimes not! Our families change - new members are born into the family and, at some time, everyone must leave. Around us we also witness constant change - the way we shop, work and travel; the way we spend our leisure time, the relative importance of education and religion - all these have changed in our lifetime, however young or old we are.

This book, using a carefully selected collection of photographs, shows some of the important changes that have taken place in the Sirhowy Valley. They show how the small shops have been superseded by the supermarket, and how the places where we work have changed, for all the collieries and ironworks have gone. They show how we've changed the way we get about. We used to walk, cycle or go by train, but today the motorcar is king. Our pleasures have changed. Gone are the days when long queues formed outside the cinemas to see the latest film or outside the Miners' Institutes, waiting to attend a Drama Festival or to dance the night away at Old English or Modern Ballroom Dancing. The only queues in this valley now are outside the pubs and the cash points. In religion and education significant changes have also occurred. Scores of chapels and churches have closed due to lack of support. They have become theatres, shops, warehouses or even homes. Children and young people now have the opportunity to become well educated, more than forty per cent setting out on a degree course. How different from the early part of the nineteenth century when seven and eight-year-old boys went underground so that their fathers could claim an extra tram of coal and girls stayed with Mam to help with the household chores.

To the older reader I am sure that this book will bring back many memories and cause you to think of what may have been the 'good old days'. Younger readers will appreciate that although they too have new problems, a great deal has changed for the better in our valley over the decades. Quite simply, as you turn the pages, I have one message - 'Enjoy what you see'.

Upper Sirhowy Valley

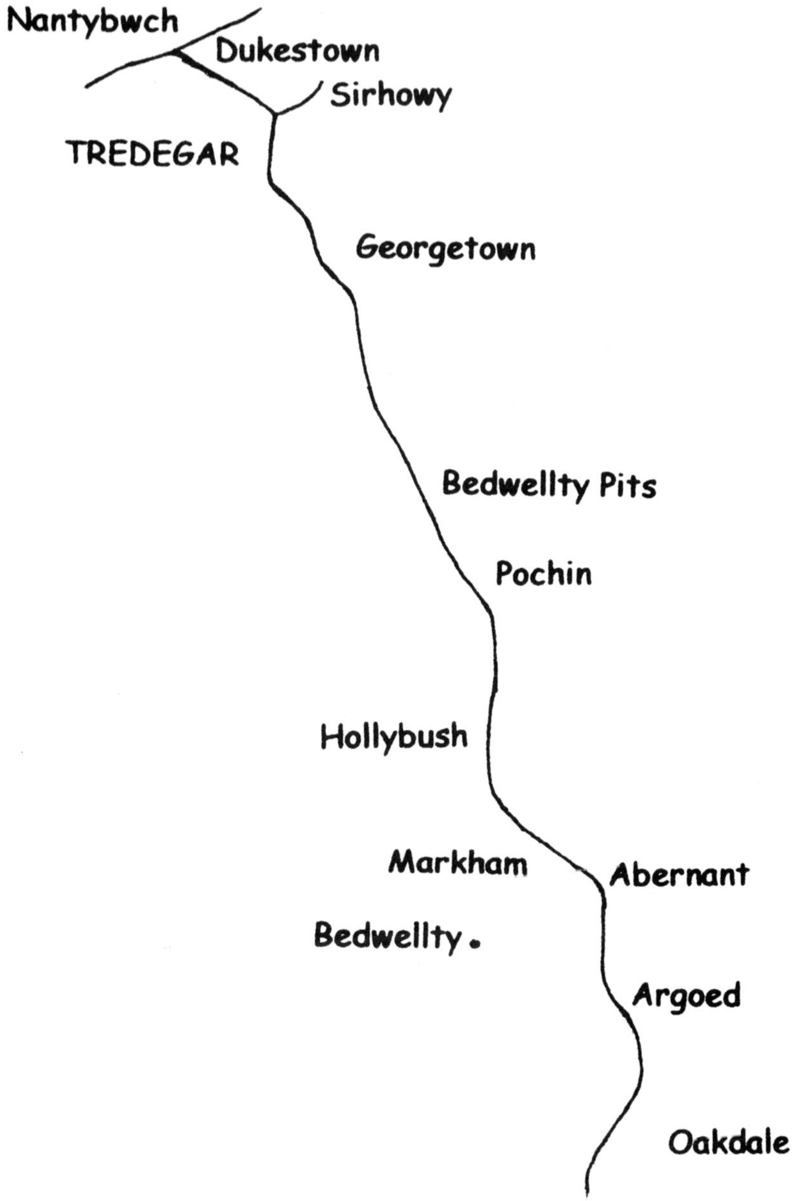

Lower Sirhowy Valley

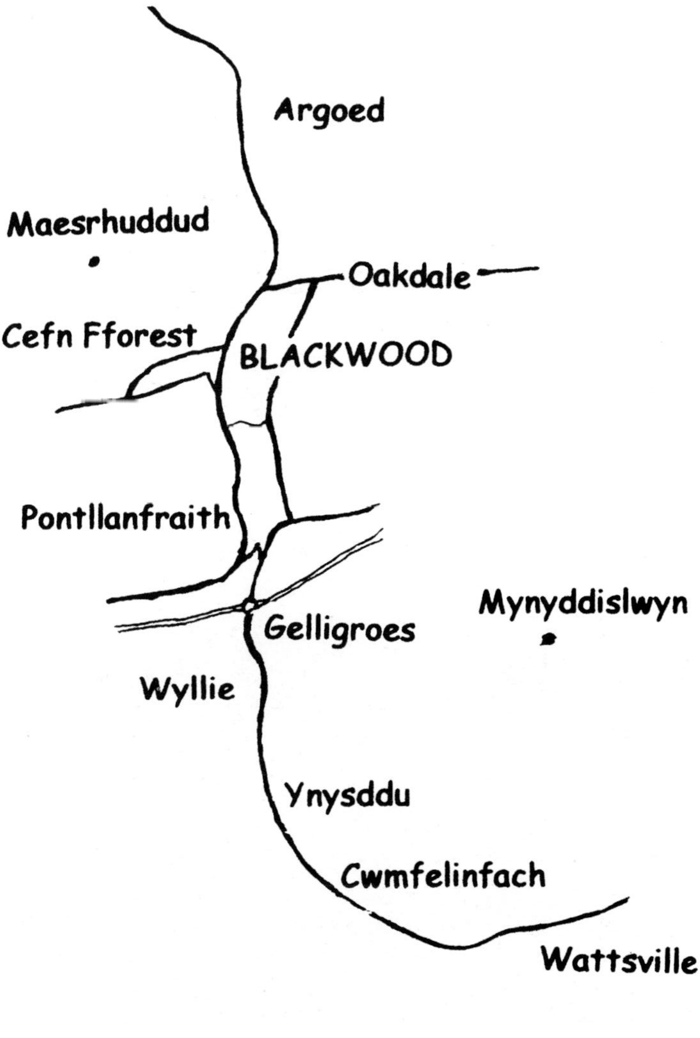

1. *The Weir and Blaen-y-cwm viaduct (Nine Arches) at Nantybwch. Trains used this viaduct on the Merthyr, Tredegar, Abergavenny line from about 1880 until it was closed in January 1958. The quality of its construction can still be admired.*

2. *In the summer, the pool area in front of the weir used to be a very popular cooling-off spot where it was even possible for children to swim. Nearby were many picnic spots. It is not such a desirable place today.*

3. *Near the site of Sirhowy Bridge, with the Registry on the left and the Thomas Richards Technical School in the distance. This is the view from Church Street on a winter's day in the 1980s.*

4. Church Street is now blocked, off except for buses but just beyond is a large roundabout linking the Tredegar by-pass with Sirhowy and Dukestown. There is now excellent visibility for road users and pedestrians in all directions.

5. The south end of Church Street leading into Tredegar. The large building on the right is the Central Surgery, to the right of which was Thomas's Temperance Bar.

6. *Apart from cars and street lighting the scene is little different.*

7. Commercial Street looking west. Note the oriel bay windows on the left and the lady in a three-wheeler wheelchair.

8. Most of the first-floor bay windows have disappeared, the telephone wires have gone underground and no sunblinds are in evidence. Is this the result of climate change?

9. Commercial Street from the west when there were private houses on the street.

10. *Private houses have now become shops and the impressive bank tower has been replaced.*

11. *The lower end of Tredegar Iron Works around 1900. The imposing building in the background is the Temperance Hall which was built in 1861.*

12. *The old terraced housing in Shop Row, Iron Street, Bridge Street and Coronation Street has been replaced and the ironworks site sports numerous small industrial units.*

13. *Looking towards Commercial Street from the top of Castle Street. The Congregational Church is on the right and a decorative water trough on the left.*

14. *The uppermost decoration of the church has been removed. Most traffic has been re-routed on to a new road to the north of the church which leads to the bus station and bypasses Commercial Street.*

15. *Looking down Castle Street towards the clock in the early 1930s. This picture shows some lovely old cars and a typical bus of the day.*

16. *The whole street looks far more prosperous than in the previous photograph.*

17. *Looking up Castle Street from the town clock towards Commercial Street. The Queen's cinema is in the distance.*

18. *The Freemasons Arms has been replaced and the road narrowed to permit parking.*

19. *The 72-foot high cast-iron Town Clock, a gift to the town from Mr R.P. Davis, the General Manager of the Tredegar Company, and his wife Mary Elizabeth. It is the symbol of Tredegar and was erected in 1858.*

20. *While the base surround is different the town clock looks virtually unchanged and is in pristine condition.*

21. *The lower end of Morgan Street with some well provisioned shops. The town clock dominates the skyline.*

22. *The porch of the old Temperance Hall, with its pillars, has disappeared and the road layout has been much improved to give more space for pedestrians.*

__23.__ The old Temperance Hall, built in 1861, below which is the old Post Office which is adjacent to the main entrance to Bedwellty Park. This office occupied the ground floor of the Masonic Hall building.

24. *The Post Office has moved to new purpose-built premises; the Workmen's Hall, formerly the Temperance Hall, has given way to a car park and the park entrance is less imposing.*

25. *The front entrance of Bedwellty House with the fountain in the background, c.1910.*

26. *The fountain is no more while the entrance to the house, now incorporating a museum, is much altered.*

27. *Lower Coronation Street, a terrace of very old houses near Bedwellty Park, in the 1960s.*

28. *The houses were condemned and pulled down. They have been replaced by the local doctors' surgery.*

29. *A truly industrial scene. Whitworth colliery and the Tredegar Iron and Coal Company's General Offices. These offices became an LCR electronics factory in 1965 but subsequently closed.*

***30.** The end of an era. All semblance of industry has disappeared. Even the TIC offices, later used as an electronics factory, have been demolished. Tredegar Comprehensive School now stands on the site.*

31. *Tredegar Grammar School, opened by Lord Tredegar in 1898, took pupils from as far afield as Blackwood. The building was used for the Middle and Upper divisions of the Comprehensive School until the new complex on the Ty Tryst/Whitworth site was ready. After this, first and second year pupils moved from the Glanhowy site until it was possible to accommodate all secondary pupils on the main site at Stable Lane.*

32. *The former grammar school site, now a secluded housing development.*

33. *The outdoor swimming baths on the upper side of Bedwellty Park, shown here on a warm summer's day. The baths were opened in 1932.*

34. *Tredegar was too cold a place for an open-air swimming baths. Indoor baths within the Leisure Centre at Stable Lane are now used, the old pool having been filled in. The original site is now used for general purposes including skateboarding.*

35. *The terraced rows of Georgetown between the wars, so reminiscent of the scenes that inspired many a Lowry painting.*

36. *The privies have gone and so have many of the chimneys. Houses have been re-roofed and rendered; several garages have been built and the whole area looks far more desirable.*

***37.** Looking south towards Bedwellty Pits in 1865. A woman carries water home while the colliery chimneys disgorge their smoke into the valley.*

38. By comparison with 1865 this part of the Sirhowy valley has become rural again.

39. *Pochin Colliery at the height of its activity. The colliery opened in 1881 and closed in 1964.*

40. *No trace of Pochin Colliery remains today. The tips have been levelled and grassed over.*

41. *Abernant Colliery, which was owned by the Bargoed Coal Company, was a working colliery from 1888 to 1932.*

42. *It is difficult to believe that a colliery, which produced some of the best smith's coal available, once stood on this site.*

43. *Markham Colliery, a subsidiary of the Tredegar Iron and Coal Company. Opened in 1912 and closed in 1985.*

44. *This site still shows the scars of industrialisation and it is only recently that it has been cleared. Its main use now appears to be as a motorcycle circuit.*

45. *The fourteenth century beacon tower of the parish church of St. Sannan, Bedwellty. This photograph is taken from the north-west.*

46. *Major restoration took place in 2002-03. Externally this included 'whitewashing' which shows how it would have looked centuries ago. It is now very much a beacon church and, on a clear day, can be seen from Pen-y-Fan, the highest peak in the Brecon Beacons.*

47. *The interior of St. Sannan's showing the 13th century central arch, the Victorian matchwood ceiling and the organ which dates from c.1900.*

48. *The restoration of 2002-03 has resulted in St. Sannan's having a beautiful oak-ribbed ceiling and now looks like it would have in medieval times. It awaits the return of the organ.*

***49.** High Street, Argoed, pre World War One showing the railway line that ran through the centre of the village. In those days the village could support a branch of Barclays Bank.*

50. *Although the railway lines are still below the surface the train has given way to the motorcar and the whole scene looks rather more appealing to the eye.*

***51.** Maesrhuddud House, the home of Captain E.D. Williams, one time High Sheriff of Monmouthshire and owner of collieries at Hollybush and Argoed.*

52. *Now set in mature gardens the house has been extended and converted into Maes Manor, an AA/RAC hotel. The courtyard, which was on the left, has become a spacious ballroom.*

53. Oakdale was built as a 'model' village with shops, a hospital, hotel, library, miners' institute, cinema and churches for all the local religious persuasions. This picture shows the bandstand on the green in the centre of the village .

54. *No sign of the bandstand now but a very nice garden is found in its place.*

55. *Oakdale Colliery, opened in 1908. In the 1930s Oakdale employed 2000 men producing one million tons of coal a year.*

56. *The colliery closed in 1990. The whole area has been cleared and restructured so that modern industry might take the place of coal.*

57. Part of the Institute in Central Avenue. It was paid for by deductions from miners' pay and opened in September 1917.

58. *The building was carefully taken down and removed to the Museum of Welsh Life, Cardiff, where it opened to the public in the 1990s. It is a perfect example of a South Wales Miners' Institute. It has been replaced by residential accommodation.*

59. The entrance to Oakdale from Crumlin. Note the roof decoration on the house to the left and the finials on the roofs of the shops and the Post Office.

60. *A Tarmacadam road surface, numerous road markings, street lighting and security cameras are now in evidence.*

61. *Blackwood Station, built 1876-78 on the LNWR line, later the London, Midland and Scottish Railway. The Carpenters Arms opposite dates from the 1830s.*

62. *All that remains from the previous scene is the wall on the left, now part of Gibbon Equipment Hire. This was formerly a boundary of Brown's foundry not to be confused with Blackwood's first foundry which stood some distance further north.*

63. *The view from the Foundry Hill c.1938. Stewart's foundry, later Trehearne's, was at the bottom of the hill on the left.*

64. *This photograph clearly illustrates the changing priorities of different times. The railway goods sheds have gone, the former main road is now a dead end and the railway line has been replaced by a new road.*

65. *Royal Stores, Cefn Fforest, between the wars. To locals it was always known as Lane's Corner.*

66. *Formerly a grocery outlet, this substantial building has been extended and converted into The Stonehouse public house.*

67. The shops, Cefn Fforest from the northern end of the complex. These few shops supplied Cefn Fforest with most of its needs.

68. All the buildings are still in use, one of them being an example of an almost extinct species - the Post Office. Additional parking has recently been added opposite.

***69.** The 'temporary' building which thousands of Blackwood schoolchildren will have used at some time. It stood for more than seventy years, being used variously as a school canteen and as classrooms.*

70. *The building has been removed and the school, which was built before the First World War, is now used as a New Deal Unit. The grounds are now tastefully laid out and well looked after.*

71. *Alfred Chaston was the principal motor dealer in the town. There were large workshops on Pentwyn Road and this showroom on the main road opposite Red Lion Row.*

72. *A major redevelopment brought an Asda supermarket to the site in 2002.*

73. A West Mon bus with driver and conductor outside the Midland Bank and Burgess the Jeweller c.1928.

74. The bank has absorbed the jeweller and become part of HSBC. The other building, which was the Crown public house and a newsagents, was taken down and replaced by Tesco's. Today it belongs to B/wise.

75. *Hall Street railway arch, built to take the new railway in 1865 - always a dangerous spot for pedestrians.*

***76.** The bridge was taken down in the 1980s. The area is now safer, and far more open and pleasant.*

77. Originally built for live performances this building became an Indoor Market before conversion into the Capitol cinema.

78. *The building stood unused for some years. It was eventually demolished and a Kwik Save supermarket erected on the site.*

79. *Looking south along Blackwood High Street in the 1950s. The extensive London Hosiery stands on the east side; Leslie Stores and the Electricity Showroom opposite.*

80. *The London Hosiery has been divided into several shops, while the Royal Oak at the end of the block and the Electricity Showroom opposite have both been demolished.*

81. *The narrow gap between the other side of this Bedwellty Urban District Council gas and electricity showroom and the business of J.D. Roberts became known as Morris Lane after the previous owner of Roberts' shop.*

82. The house and shop were taken down to widen the lane into a proper road and a new electricity showroom built on the ground to the left. This was removed to widen to road yet further when the new shopping precinct was built in the 1990s.

83. Woodward's the butchers in the days when it was permitted to hang raw meat outside the shop in the open air.

84. *The displays outside the same premises in the twenty-first century are now floral and more colourful.*

85. *An example of cottages that probably date from the founding of Blackwood by John Moggridge of Woodfield Park in the early part of the nineteenth century.*

86. *Enough time has elapsed for a sapling to grow into a substantial tree. Geo. Jones's, which replaced the cottages, has become a fitness centre and Bridge Street Garage has been built with access from Thorncombe Road.*

87. *The three-storey Parrot Hotel at the bottom end of the High Street. This was the largest hotel in the town and was used for numerous community activities.*

88. The hotel has been replaced by an impressive and much used Caerphilly Borough Branch Library. It also doubles as an internet centre.

89. *Entrance into Blackwood in the days of the horse and cart, muddy tracks and gas lighting. Note the buckets on the edge of the pavement. These would have contained ashes and other household rubbish.*

90. *Still a peaceful scene but far more amenable. A petrol station, formerly Love and Evans' Garage, has replaced the cottages in the distance.*

***91.** A view of Blackwood from the east showing the single storey prefabricated houses along Albany Road. The prefabs were erected in the late 1940s to help relieve the pressure on housing resulting from the war.*

92. *Significant development has taken place as far as the eye can see. Every conceivable space has now been taken for building.*

93. A typical local farming scene from yesteryear. Mr. and Mrs. Lloyd in the yard with some of their stock at Penllwynbach Farm.

94. *The importance of farming decreased as more and more people came into the area. Today, this former farmland is the site of Blackwood Police Station.*

95. *A coal train at Pontllanfraith High Level in the 1960s. By this time the line was being used less and less so the down-line was removed and the up-line used for traffic in both directions.*

96. *The road is now much wider permitting car parking outside the shops and stops for down-valley buses opposite.*

97. The level crossing and signal box at Pontllanfraith taken from the north. This was on the LNWR line which linked Nantybwch, above Tredegar, with Newport.

98. *The train has given way to the motor car. Road level is now much higher as indicated by the house on the right.*

99. Looking towards Pontllanfraith bottom station. The Great Western line from Pontypool to Swansea is on the left.

100. *The railway cutting has been filled in to provide half of a short section of dual carriageway.*

101. *The first version of a very small St. Augustine's Church. The church dates from 1870.*

102. *St. Augustine's was doubled in size in the early 1920s and a west porch added in 1995. Since the demise of the railway they have an extremely large car park on the adjacent former station site.*

103. *The Greyhound, a large inn much in evidence in 1839 as a Chartist meeting place.*

104. *The former hotel is now a veterinary centre under the guiding hand of veterinary surgeon Barrie Williams. There is residential accommodation above.*

105. *S.D. Roberts & Co., one of the first large local garages. This picture shows early cars which ran on solid tyres. Note the two-digit telephone number.*

106. *The building, though much changed, is easily recognisable and still a Ford garage.*

107. *Ivor Street, Pontllanfraith, viewed from the south, which was a dead end. At this time the main route down the valley was along Gelligroes Road.*

108. *Today, Ivor Street is part of the main road from Pontllanfraith to Newport.*

109. *St. Tudor's Church, Mynyddislwyn showing quite clearly that it was at one time a white-washed hilltop church.*

110. *The chimney stack has gone, the roof has been completely restructured, and the building tastefully restored inside and out.*

111. *The Mill at Gelligroes early in the last century when it was still a working mill.*

112. *No longer a working mill, externally little has changed. Even the Victorian postbox, just around the left hand corner, remains.*

113. *High Street, Ynysddu, when all boys wore long trousers and men wore caps, bowlers or straw hats.*

114. *It is no longer necessary to carry water, but it is now quite difficult to see the whole of the road surface. People now have other things to do than stand around on the street. The Post Office is on the left hand side. It moved from Commercial Street several decades ago.*

115. *A view of Stanley Square, Cwmfelinfach, when it was a shopping street. The main valley road is beyond the houses.*

116. *All the shops have gone but the buildings remain. The top shop front, just beyond the gap, has been most stylishly converted into a house.*

117. *French's three shops in Maindee Road, Cwmfelinfach. The shop on the left was for men, the one on the right for ladies and the central one for a variety of goods including footwear. The idea seemed to be that men and women were segregated when looking for clothes!*

118. *Supermarkets and out-of-town shopping have resulted in many local shops, as here, being turned into residential accommodation. Mr. Bunnie Jones walks past the houses he remembers as the photograph opposite.*

119. *An old picture of Wattsville with its industrial buildings and terraced houses surmounted by their smoking chimneys.*

120. *An altogether cleaner looking landscape, with more trees and houses.*

Acknowledgements

Several people have helped in the production of this book, through their willingness to give me of their time and to share photographs and information. In particular I would like to thank Lyn Pinney for his help in Tredegar, Nicholas and Gwenda Lanagan for two superb old photographs of Blackwood High Street, John Moore, Mike Johnson and Doug Gilchrist. John Watkins was once again kind enough to peruse the draft copy and made several useful suggestions. For this I am most grateful.

Above all I would like to thank Gwilym Davies and Malcolm Thomas of Old Bakehouse Publications. They initiated *The Sirhowy Valley; As It Was and As It Is*, and have kept a careful eye on it at each stage of its production. May I also thank all the staff at the publishers who have always been most courteous and helpful, and who have made many worthwhile suggestions.

The author would very much welcome the loan of any unpublished photographs, memorabilia, etc., from readers who might wish to see the material included in the next *Blackwood Yesterday* book. He may be contacted through the publishers at the address found at the front of this book.